HOW TO BOOST YOUR WIFI SIGNAL

Updated for 2021

Get the WI -fi you need all over your house

ABOUT THIS BOOK

You come home from work, and you want to get online and check out a few things before dinner. The wi-fi connection is slow, and you get frustrated and upset. I know exactly what you feel like. It is so frustrating when things do not work right when you want to use them. I am the same way. I have found some answers and will share them with you.

Almost everyone these days have home Internet service. It is a big part of our everyday lives starting at a young age. Like most things, when the Internet is working well, all is great. When the Internet stops working well, it is very frustrating.

This book is for the average person who wants to get the most from your Internet service and Wi-Fi. There is not a lot of deep tech info in this book. There is enough technical information for you to understand how everything works. Enough so you can make it work better. This book is for advice, tips, and techniques for regular non tech people. Use these tips so you can get the best out of your internet access and wi-fi with less frustration.

To have good internet everywhere in your home is something we all want. It is not something that regularly happens. There are many things that affect wi-fi, and it is not always what we want. There are things you can do to improve your service. Good wi-fi is important and can affect many things in your life.

As more people get on the Internet the more congested it gets. There are limits to how many people can use the service at the same time over the same pathways. Like a highway, the pathways get congested. Delivering the service to your house is the job of the ISP that you pay for your service.

Many of them are working all the time to get the service to you better and faster. Once it gets into your house, it is your Internet connection and wi-fi that is the biggest issue. There are things you can do to make it work the best it can be, so you can use it everywhere in your house.

I will go over the pieces of the network you need to understand and how they work. I will give you enough information, so you know what you need to know. What you need to do to get great internet and the best Wi-Fi throughout your home network.

This advice, techniques and tips in this book will help you get the best performance out of your

Internet. To improve your life and make it less frustrating. I tried many things to improve my Wi-Fi. I will share what I did to fix the problems and how you can do the same in your house.

Follow the links throughout the book if you want to learn more about the types of devices, otherwise follow the tips to get great internet.

TABLE OF CONTENTS

INTERNET SPEED

What is Internet speed? People confuse megabit and megabyte all the time. The term's byte and bit are different. A bit is ⅛ of a byte.

50 megabits per second (mbps) of Internet speed mean you are getting 6.25 megabytes per second. Gigabit Internet is 1000mbps. At the best speed, you will get 125 megabytes per second. So, you know the correct terms. If your Internet speed is a 12, 25, 50 100, or 200, it is not megabytes; it is megabits.

You can get Internet speeds from dial up, which is .056mbps. You can get up to two gbps at the top end with fiber. Avoid dial up, it is like having no service. The best area of speed for most people that will work as you want, is in the 200 to 400mbps range. The speed you need depends on what you do and how many devices are online at one time.

If you are doing a lot on Wi-Fi, not direct wired, the speed you get from Wi-Fi at the devices is the critical speed. While a wired speed is important, the speeds at the connection points are more essential for getting the device to work for you.

If you are getting a solid 25mbps at the device, and you are connecting on the Wi-Fi with one device, you can do most anything you want. If you are real time gaming or streaming several devices at the same time, 25mbps will be too slow.

If you are not getting the speed where you use your Wi-Fi, you will need to make improvements. If you do not, you will not be happy with your connection.

The speed you get from your ISP is the speed at your modem. To get a good speed test for what you are getting from your ISP, you must test direct through an ethernet cable from your router to a PC.

When you run a speed test, the results are mbps. **Speedtest.net** is one of the most popular and one I use often. Another one I like is **fast.com**. There are apps for phones and tablets as well. There are good other speed tests available, fast.com is my go-to now, it is quick and easy to use.

TYPES OF INTERNET

There are different Internet connections you can get. Quality varies by type. The speed of the Internet service you get to your house can be much higher than the signal you are getting on Wi-Fi. Because of things that affect it. There can be a significant loss of signal over Wi-Fi. We will get into why the losses occur later in the book.

Dial Up. This is the worst type of connection. If you only check email, you may still use this service. Even emailing a picture can make dial up unusable. Dial-up internet service is like riding a tricycle on the Autobahn. You can do it, but it is a bad idea.

Satellite internet. This service they say can now give you speed up to 15mbps. The plus side is you can get service where there are no other options. The downside is it is expensive to set up and has a high monthly cost. There are also low data caps on how much you can use it. This is a last resort if you cannot get anything else, and you need Internet service.

DSL. This is much better than dial up and can give speeds up to 30 to 60mbps. That is fast enough for most people and doing most things if you can get that speed. If you are on a wired network, dsl may be good enough for most things you want to do.

Speeds on dsl can be unreliable. The signal is coming to you over the phone wire that was never designed to send data. The signal can also be much lower depending on how far your house is from the phone company central office.

As I stated, you will lose speed if you send your signal through the air with Wi-Fi. You will not get the 30 to 40mbps on wi-fi far from the router and with any obstacles blocking the signal, it will go down even more.

Some DSL ISP's use fiber as the backbone of their system, if the fiber comes into your house, you can get the best speeds. If the signal still comes to your house on the phone wires, you are limited by that old technology.

Cable Internet service. This is the most common and it is readily available for most people. Cable internet uses fiber as the backbone of the system. Then changes to coax cable for the last connection going to your house from the fiber network. You can get speeds up to two gigabits per second in some areas, but at least 200 mbps from some cable providers. The signal can be less in places where you are a long way from the fiber backbone.

Cable will give you the best signal for the most economical cost in most areas. Coax can carry a much better signal than phone wire under almost all situations.

Fiber to your house. This is the best Internet connection you can get. This service can give you in some areas now over 1 gbps speeds. It could go much faster when the modem and router technology catches up and is affordable. Gigabit speed can handle anything you need to do at this time. In most cases, this is the most expensive option. It may be worth the cost if you need speed and consistency in that range.

Remember you need the fiber to your house and throughout your house to get the best speed possible. The signal will only be as good as the weakest part of your connection.

It is like a water line. If there is a 12-inch water line going down your street and the line coming into your house is a 2-inch line. The water then runs through a ½ inch pipe to get to your faucet. You are only at best going to get what the ½ pipe can deliver, not the volume of the 12-inch line in the street. Your Internet signal works much the same way.

3G or 4G wi-fi hotspot from a cell phone carrier. This system can get your speed into the same area as good dsl service. This is also not a great option most times. Because of data usage limits and cost, it is also not a good price point in most situations. However, it is a viable option if nothing else is available.

INTERNET AND WIFI

Internet is the connection your modem makes to the outside world. Internet lets you use your home network to access the rest of the world. The Internet is a giant network of millions of smaller networks connected. The image below is a small representation of what the Internet looks like. There are millions of Neighbors.

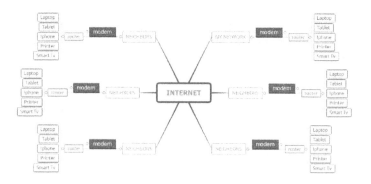

Your router with hard-wired and Wi-Fi signal creates your own closed loop. This group of private devices make up your home network. The best service you will get from your network to the outside world is being hardwired into your router with an ethernet cable.

When you use Wi-Fi, you are sending the signal through the air. The signal must compete with similar signals from other devices. Devices like cordless phones, microwave ovens, Bluetooth, and others. These all interfere with your Wi-Fi signal.

Things in your house like metal, mirrors, steel cabinets and desks, all hurt wi-fi. Even mesh with plaster in the walls can stop the signal. There are a lot of obstacles to wi-fi in your house. Distance is also working against your Wi-Fi signal going throughout your house.

If you set up a peer-to-peer network, every device on your home network can talk to each of the other devices on your network. My printer connected to my network will print documents from my laptop or desktop or tablet. I can also print pictures from my phone to the printer on my network.

You can also set up a file server on your network. You can use the file server to store anything you want to access from any other device in your network. You can also open this up to the rest of the world and share it if you want. Be careful if you do this.

If you plan on having more devices hard-wired, there are devices called switches or hubs. You can use a switch to give you more ports to run wires to your router. Like an electric power strip, you can plug many devices into the strip, and then into one outlet. They are like power strips for your router.

You can hardwire devices up to 100 meters away without big signal loss. This is the leading solution for the best coverage. The problem is getting the cables from the router to where you want them to go. If you are building a new house, it is easy; you can run Ethernet cable through the walls to all parts of your house.

If you are not building a new house, the options are less. You do not want cables lying on the floor throughout your house. This means you will use Wi-Fi for many of your Internet connections. Many devices we use can only connect wireless; they must use wi-fi.

Wi-Fi is something we all use and need, and it can be one of our biggest frustrations in our everyday life. You want it to work. Wi-Fi that drops or buffers when you are trying to do something is very frustrating. I read that even the White House has issues with dropping signals and losing the connection. The more people that use the internet, the worse the problem will be.

Many people are not sure what the difference is between wi-fi and the Internet. Because of the devices you use, many of you only use Wi-Fi and are never directly plugged into a router. This makes getting a strong consistent Wi-Fi signal critical. Being able to do the things you need to do on the Internet requires good wi-fi.

Internet access is what you get with a modem coming into your home. If you only use a direct connection, you do not even need Wi-Fi. My desktop computer is where I do a lot of my work and writing. This is on an ethernet connection. The direct connection is a great solid connection of 400 mbps.

Like most of you. I do many things with Wi-Fi; much of it is because my phone and tablets cannot connect with a wired connection. I try to use a wired connection whenever I can because it is a much faster and consistent connection.

Most people in the U.S. and throughout the world use the Internet daily. They use if for much of their entertainment and everyday living. Intermittent and weak Wi-Fi connections are getting worse because of overcrowded networks. Because of the Covid-19 pandemic many people are now working from home as well. This puts more strain on the system and makes a solid connection even more critical.

The problems will continue to get worse if we do nothing. Almost every home in your neighborhood has several people online. Each of them has many devices they are using to access the Internet.

It is kind of like an interstate highway system. Making it so crowded is that every household has everyone in the house using the highway, even small kids. And many of the people using the highway are driving several vehicles at one time on this highway. A computer, a tablet, a phone, and many televisions in the house.

If you live in an apartment, it will be even worse. There are likely to be more problems because of interference from other routers in the area. The overlapping networks cause more interference with each other. If you live in an apartment, good wi-fi is more critical.

The more hard-wired connections the better for avoiding interference. Each wireless router puts out a spherical signal that overlaps each other. As you add more, they interfere more and more with each other. Multiple overlapping signals from all directions will cause problems with each other.

Think of how many devices you are using. Multiply that by everyone in your neighborhood and everyone in your city. It creates the need for a big highway system. Then you add in the need for more speed because everyone is driving faster.

We need more fast lanes so we can get past the people in the slow lanes. It all takes more lanes. Many cell networks are also using the Wi-Fi networks for cell phone operation. This is adding more congestion and the need for more lanes for traffic.

Wi-Fi in home networks operates in two frequencies. 2.4 ghz and 5ghz. There is a 6 ghz band that is now available. The 6 ghz is quick but it is not usable unless you have devices that support wi-fi 6E. There are very few devices that support this now, but it will make things in the future better.

A huge amount of traffic is operating in the 2.4 ghz range. Accessing the 5ghz band on your router and your devices will increase speed and wi-fi stability. There is much less traffic on the 5 ghz highway, and more lanes to drive in. Many devices still do not support the 5 ghz band currently.

What causes Wi-Fi loss and signals to drop is that the data packets on the highway crash. When they collide, both packets that crashed stop communicating for a time. They must stop while they fix the damage.

The more crashes they have, the longer the time it takes before they can move again. The high congestion in many areas has made it almost impossible to send data on the 2.4ghz band in peak times. They are crashing constantly. Many wireless carriers and many manufacturers do not recommend even using the 2.4 ghz band anymore.

Older 802.11b wireless devices can also slow down your other devices. The new routers are backward compatible to make sure all Wi-Fi devices will work. The older devices could only work one device at a time. The newer routers must stop everything while they process the old device. Most older devices can only work one device at a time. This slows your entire network down while it waits for the old device to finish.

The best way to stop this is to use 5 ghz band for all your newer devices. The older devices will work on the 2.4 ghz only. They cannot access the 5ghz band, so they will slow down the devices connected to 5ghz. It will make you wait for the slower devices to communicate. One place this can come into play in a big way is if you have new tv's and computers that can use the faster band, but you have an old cell phone that can only work at the slower 2.4 ghz. If someone is surfing on the phone, it slows down the entire network. Most camera's also work at the slower rate.

Most new devices can access the 5 ghz wi-fi band. It is much better to use the 5 ghz for most things with devices that can use it. You need a 5ghz band on your router to access the 5ghz band. Look for a dual band router if renting or buying a router.

With my old setup, when I was working on my laptop in the living room, I could get a good steady signal at 30 mbps on the 5ghz band. In the same spot using the 2.4 ghz I could get about 10 mbps. The 2.4ghz is up and down and sometimes will stop, this is because of the packets crashing from high traffic. Even the 5 ghz signal would slow or stop at times.

I lived in a townhouse and there are many networks I can see from my house. They are all competing for the same highway lanes. There is only one other network I can see from my house that is using the 5 ghz highway, and the 5 ghz has many more lanes to use. It is much better to drive in the 5 ghz lanes.

Many people now are using range extenders. They help get the wi-fi signal to places where you are having problems getting service. This has made the issue even worse sometimes. The extender creates more interference from one area into other areas. There is now another signal interfering. The signal networks are overlapping with other networks. Look at the picture below, every extender adds another signal to interfere with the existing signals.

You have a router that is putting out a signal in a sphere around the router. Say the signal goes out 100 feet. You have another router from a neighbor, their router is 50 feet from your router. This router is putting out a spherical signal 100 feet. You have more and more routers doing the same thing. They are all causing interference with each other because they overlap. The more routers in the area, the

more they cause each other problems. Keep adding
circles to the same size picture and you see what the
problem is.

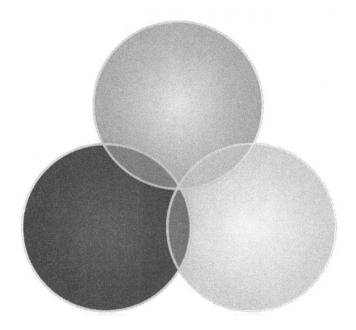

The point of telling you all this is that wi-fi will get
worse before it gets better, at least in the 2.4 ghz
band. To make it work for you, you will need
everything hardwired and not use wi-fi. That is
impossible, so you need to get the best wi-fi setup
and the most efficient wi-fi you can get. I
researched and will share with you the best tips and

tricks for you to get the most out of your Internet and wi-fi.

HOME NETWORKING

Some Networking things to know.

It is good to reboot your modem and router.
Most people are not aware that you should reboot your modem and router. It is good for the device health, for updates and to get the junk out. Try to do it on a schedule. Some people recommend doing it every couple of days. What I found is a good timeframe is reset it once a week so you will remember to do it.

I reset mine on Sunday. Because I am always home on Sunday night, and it is the start to the week. I am not saying you must reboot every week, but it hurts nothing, and it only takes a couple of minutes. You can do it while your eating dinner or something that you are not using any internet. In the summer I do it from my phone on the way home from the cabin. If you do it remotely you do not have to wait for it, and it is done when you get there.

<u>What is a wireless router?</u> A wireless router is a device to hook to a network that is the network controller. You connect wired and wireless devices

to the network with the router. The router has wired ports to plug in wired devices. A wireless router also sends out a signal on the 2.4 ghz and the 5 ghz band with a dual band wireless router.

What is an access point? An access point is a device to connect to the network that allows other devices to connect through wi-fi. It is not the same thing as a wireless router. A wireless router is an access point. Not all access points are wireless routers, it can be a wired access point only.

Another way to see the difference. Think of a place that has free Wi-Fi for customers. There is a wireless router they can access for the business. There is an access point separated from the business access. That access point lets the customers access the internet on a different subnetwork.

Wireless repeater. A wireless repeater, or a range extender. Is a device that takes the signal from a router and sends it out as the same network. This extends the range of the wireless signal to make the network usable farther from the router. Many modern wireless routers contain a repeater mode.

Wireless Bridge. This device works kind of the opposite of an access point. The bridge connects to a wireless network. It allows wired devices to plug in with wires and access the network. Many modern wireless routers also contain a bridge mode.

Wireless network adapter. This is a device that plugs into a usb port or a card installed in the computer. It lets devices without wireless built into them access the network. The wi-fi circuit is controlled through the adapter. Not used much anymore, most devices have wi-fi built in.

Modem. A modem is a device that allows your network to connect with the rest of the world through the internet. That comprises millions of other networks connecting through modems you can tap into. That is how you get the information and entertainment you are looking for.

MAKING SURE YOUR ROUTER IS SECURE
One of the most important things to do for security is to keep your firmware updated. Most router manufacturers update the firmware to fix bugs and security issues. It's a good idea to sign up to the mfg.'s blog or follow them on Facebook. That way you will know when they put out firmware updates for your router.

How to update the router firmware.

- Look at the bottom or back of the router. Copy the model and version number.
- Go to the manufacturer's website and go to their support page. Find the latest firmware for your router. Download the file to your computer.
- Locate the default gateway and ip address for the router. To find this go to the start menu or the search window on windows 10. Type in cmd. When the command box opens, type in ipconfig. Look for default gateway or ip address and write it down.
- Type the default gateway or ip address into the window of your Internet browser. This will pull up the router web interface.
- Look for update or upgrade firmware under the administration or management tab.
- Choose upload file and upload the file to the router.

Some ISP'S do this for you if you rent the modem router from them. Here is a quote from the Xfinity support site. "One advantage of renting a Xfinity XFi Gateway is that we regularly update our firmware automatically, so you don't have to check for new updates."

This is important so you have the best security and you do not have to go through the steps above and you do not have to remember to do this. Check with your ISP.

Change password.

Make sure you change the password from the default password on your router. This is also something to do if your network is slow. If you go onto your network and look at the devices that are there, you may see many devices you do not know what they are or have not been used for a long time. Doing a password reset will knock off ever device on the network. You will have to go back in on each device and reconnect with the new password, but you will know exactly what devices are using your network and all the old devices will be gone. Changing the password occasionally will help clean up your network and make it safer and faster.

Secure your Wi-Fi.

Use the wpa/ wpa2 encryption. Not the wep. And use a passphrase that someone cannot figure out.

Disable UPnP in the router web page.

Log out of the router web page when you are done configuring it.

SET UP HOME NETWORK

A wired connection from your router is always the best way to set up your network. It is not possible sometimes. Most people do not want Ethernet cables running all over the house. When setting up a wired network you may run out of ports on the router. You can add a switch to get more connections to the router. Switches come in sizes up to 52 ports. Prices go up as number of ports goes up. You can get a 5 port for $25 to $30.

If you need to add more than one switch, it is best to connect each switch to a port of the router. You can go from a switch to another switch, but each time, you add the chance of noise and signal corruption. It is best not to chain them together if you can avoid it. However, it is still better to chain them together for a wired connection, instead of using Wi-Fi in most situations if possible.

To set up your home network with Wi-Fi, the best setup would be to place the router in the physical center of the house at a raised level. We all know it is impractical or not workable to set up that way most of the time.

Many of your set-ups are like mine. There is the modem and router in my rec room downstairs in one corner of the house. My setup is like that because that is where the wiring comes into the house. I have an ethernet cable running out of site to my office where I have a switch, that I can connect my personal computers and my work computer for the fastest speed. I want my desktop and my work computer plugged in direct to get the best connection.

At my previous place, the setup was different. The modem and router were in an upstairs office in a corner of the house. My desktop was there, and it worked great there; always a good connection and I get 360 to 430 mbps. The Wi-Fi down in the living room on the other side of the house was sketchy. I could sometimes get 40mbps, other times 20mbps, even as low as 5 mbps. There was little consistency.

This is the situation that happens in many houses all over the country. It is common. How do you fix this and get the best Internet connection to get what you need for the things you want and need to do?

What are things you should not do when setting up Wi-Fi?
There are many things that will affect a Wi-Fi signal. Obstacles are one of them. Wi-Fi will go through walls, but some materials stop a lot of Wi-Fi signals. Cement, brick, and steel will kill a Wi-Fi signal. This includes chimneys and fireplaces.

Mirrors are signal reflectors. If your router is near a large mirror, there will be no signal getting to devices on the other side of the mirror. Plaster with chicken wire type mesh in them, will kill almost all wi-fi outside the room where the router is located.

Water is also bad for Wi-Fi signals. Putting your router near an aquarium or behind it will also kill your signal in that direction.

Other things that make a big difference on Wi-Fi are electronic devices. Many devices use similar frequencies as wi-fi. Cordless phones, microwaves, and Bluetooth signals are bad. Many other devices with motors in them will generate noise and interference that is also bad.

Do not put your router inside a cabinet or closet. Put the router in a place away from most other electronic devices. Even remote controls can interfere with your Wi-Fi signal.

Do not put the router next to a metal desk or cabinet unless it is in a direction you do not want or need a signal to go. If there is a metal cabinet on an outside wall, you can put the router in front of the cabinet. You will not get the signal going outside the house on that side, but it does not affect the signal going other directions. It may even send more signal the way you want it to go.

What are things you should do?
I read this tip on CNet. I never tried it, but the article said it may help direct the signal a bit in the direction you want. You can do a couple of things that can help and cost little. You can cut off the end of an aluminum can drill a hole in the side and put your router antenna through the hole. This will act as a directional antenna for your Wi-Fi. This is a trick if your router setup is on one side of your house, or in a basement. You can point the open end of the can in the direction you want to direct the signal. You need external antennas on the router to do this.

If your router has an internal antenna, you can take a piece of cardboard long enough to go around most of the device. Cover the cardboard with aluminum foil. This will stop the signal from going into the wall behind the router. It will direct the signal toward the area you want the signal to go. These are not great solutions but can give you a better signal and direct your Wi-Fi signal where you want it to go.

This may sound silly but if you look on the internet, there are many reliable websites that give advice on making some type of deflector to send more signal in a direction you want it to go. If you have your router on an outside wall, give it a try, many people say it works.

If your router has external antennas. Point the antenna's different directions for better coverage. If it is a two-antenna router, one should be horizontal and one vertical. If it is a three-antenna router. One horizontal, one vertical and the other a different setting. Change the third one and see which way having it will give you the best signal. Think of the signal from each antenna coming out in a sphere around the antenna. If you want the signal to go up or down from the router, alter the direction of the antennas to get better coverage.

Reboot your router. This is sometimes the only thing you need to do if your Internet has slowed down or is intermittent. If there are networks close to you rebooting the router can also help. Rebooting will pick a different channel and cut interference to your network.

If many people around you are on the same channel, everyone's service is slower. They interfere because of it. Most new routers will pick the best channel when they start up. So, a reboot can help by picking a different channel with less interference.

HOW DOES WIFI WORK

The way Wi-Fi works is the Internet signal comes from the modem to the router. The router sends out the wi-fi signal you connect to. One of the important things about Wi-Fi is that you get it set up right and protect it.

There are gateway devices that the modem and router are in the same box. They are better for some reasons but not better for others. If there is a power outage, or you reset your modem, you will need to reset your router also if they are separate devices. If your device is a gateway with both in the same box, restarting the box will restart both pieces.

The downside is most of them have internal antennas. They do not have as good a signal output as a separate router with external antennas. External antennas on a router will give you a better output signal than an internal antenna. Also, a router with external antennas that are longer will give you better signal. This can make a huge difference. If you have a router with external antennas and they are short, you can upgrade to longer antennas to get better signal output without getting a new router.

How to set up your wireless gateway.

- Look at the label on the gateway device.
- Record the network name (ssid) and the network key. You can also just take a picture of the plate with your phone and you will have all the info. Click on the wireless connection icon in the lower-right part of your screen. Pick the network on the label on the gateway.
- Enter the network key or password.
- Click on ok or connect.
- Test your Internet connection by typing in a valid website or click on a web link in your bookmarks.
- Open a Web browser and type **http://10.0.0.1** in the address line.
- Create a password. It must contain uppercase and lowercase, be at least 8 characters and at least one number.
- Re Enter password again and write it down where you keep your passwords, so you know where to find it when you need it.
- Change the name of the network so you can identify it.

- Select the encryption method and pick WPAWPA2-PSK (TKIP/AE).
- Enter a unique network password in the network password space. Make it something you can remember but something someone cannot figure out. It should contain both upper- and lower-case letters, and at least one number. Do not forget to record the new password.
- Go to the wireless icon and look for the network you changed your network name too.
- Go to each of the devices you want to connect to the network. Pick your network and enter the password and connect each of your devices.
- All done.

- If you have Xfinity as your ISP, you can download the Xfinity app to your phone or tablet, and it will help you get it all set up without doing the steps in the above section. You can also do this online at their support website.

OPTIMIZING ROUTER

Operating your router to the best of its ability is a key need for the best Internet and Wi-Fi service in your house. Buying the optimum router for your needs is where you should do this.

What router should I get?
There are hundreds of choices in the market. You need to decide what you want the router to do. Look for the one that will do it at the best price for you. Your ISP may supply your modem router to you in a single device. Check with them and make sure it is the latest one you can get. You should be able to upgrade to the latest available for no charge if you rent it from the ISP.

If you are using your own router, then the decision making can make a big difference in the performance you get. The most basic and easiest to decide router is not a wireless router. If you use a single computer and only use it in one spot in your house. If you do not have a smartphone or a tablet you use on the internet, then you do not need a wireless router.

If this is you, you are in a tiny group of people. Almost everyone has a smartphone or a tablet, or a Kindle or laptop they use on Wi-Fi in various parts of their house. Wi-Fi is important for most people. If you use wi-fi, then you need a wireless router. The wireless router supplies the Wi-Fi signal throughout your house to those devices.

What you may use Wi-Fi for. Searching the Internet on your smartphone. Searching for addresses and phone numbers. Getting books to reading devices. Listening to music, playing games online with your gaming device. Streaming video to your TV from Netflix, or other streaming services. Security cameras, sharing photos and more. The list will continue to increase with more devices invented. If you do any of these things, you will need a wireless router.

Wireless routers.
The higher the price of the router, the more features on it. This does not mean it will give you better performance. After you decide the features you need. Go to a big seller website like Amazon or Newegg and read the reviews. See what the people

that are using the ones you like say about them. Furthermore, read reviews on websites that review routers. After you have this info, make your decision based on that info.

Single or dual band. If you are buying a router, the cost of getting a dual band over a single band in most cases is worth it. Single band routers are very inexpensive and can be just the ticket for some situations. If it is your main router though, go with a dual band. Connecting to the 5 ghz Wi-Fi can cut a lot of problems with Wi-Fi signals. With most wireless devices that are newer than 3 or 4 years old, you can access the 5 ghz Wi-Fi. The 5 ghz band is faster and has less interference, but there is a shorter range. I recommend you use the 5ghz any time you can.

Another consideration for a dual band router is your own band for your home network. Example. If you work at home, or if you want part of your Internet separate from the rest, it can be useful. Say you have a teenager that does a lot of online gaming, this uses a lot of bandwidth. When he is playing, you may not have enough bandwidth for simple things you want to do online.

Plug his game system directly with an Ethernet cable if you can. If not, you could make sure his game system only connects to the 5ghz band. Then you can use the 2.4ghz band for what you need to do, and you will not slow down because of his gaming. Or set it up vice versa if you need the faster speed you can only let your kids on the 2.4 and not the 5ghz.

You can set each up with different passwords, so they cannot get on your band if they do not know the password. There can be many users who will not compete for the faster band if you do not want them too.

There are two types of dual band routers on the market. Selectable or simultaneous. The simultaneous dual band router has twice the bandwidth of a selectable dual band. You can operate both the 2.4 ghz and the 5 ghz bands at the same time.

Selectable is much better if using a high-bandwidth device only. If using an Xbox or other online gaming system, you can select the 5 ghz to gaming and use all your bandwidth for that one device. One more consideration when looking at routers. The simultaneous will be the best for most people and most situations.

Speed is another consideration when buying a router. Router mfg. will put a speed on the router. This speed is theoretical. You may reach it in a perfect environment, but something you will never get in your house. When you look at the mfg.'s speed rating, think most likely the best you can get about half of that speed or less.

You also will not get more speed than what is coming in. If you pay for 250 mbps Internet service, you cannot get 300mbps speed from your router. A good router will get you about 50 to 75% of what is coming in, out to wi–fi under most conditions. A not so good router will give you less.

So, if you are wanting to watch Netflix on your TV on the other side of your house from your router. Your Internet is 25 mbps service coming to your house. You are going to be getting a speed of 10mbps or less at the TV. Netflix recommends 10 mb at least for HD streaming at the TV. If you can plug it direct, there will be no problem.

Other considerations are, how long do you want this router to be a good device. As with most electronics, the technology keeps changing. Do you want to buy another router in a year? Are your needs going to change for you or other people in your household?

As with most electronics, I recommend you get the best one you can afford that will do the things you want. Look ahead also, choose for now and for the next few years. Get at least an 802.11n router. The new 802.11ac routers have some cool features that are worth a look.

The newest beamforming technology will direct the signal to where you are using it. This is a benefit worth looking into. The router does the same thing that the can with a hole over the antenna does. The beamforming shoots the signal to where you are using it.

The Wi-Fi signal from your router transmits in a spherical pattern from the antenna. The signal will be the same strength in all directions from the router with nothing blocking. The beamforming technology will change the way the signal goes out.

If you are in the next room using Wi-Fi and no one else is on your network. The router will point the strongest signal at you where you are using the Wi-

Fi. This will give you the best signal possible where you are. It will also not waste the signal throughout the rest of the area around the antenna.

Routers and blocked signal are the cause of most wi-fi issues that people experience. The problem of Internet connection dropping on Wi-Fi is a big problem. Much of this comes from channel saturation in areas where there are too many networks.

Crashing of data packets is the cause of drops in high congested areas at high congestion times. The issue is too many people trying to use the same frequency at the same time. Remember when you were in school and the bell rang, and all 25 kids try to get through the door at the same time? That is what happens all the time in busy internet areas.

In my townhouse, I could see 13 networks. Of those 13 only one other network is on the 5ghz band, all the rest are 2.4ghz. The 5ghz was much better for me when there is a lot of traffic.

Another cause is cheap routers. This is not a place to skimp and go for the cheapest router you can get. You will not need the most expensive, but do not go for the cheapest. There are routers ranging in price from $25 up to $500. Look at the features and see what you need it to do. Read reviews by customers, and by the big online sites that review routers. Websites like cnet and topreviews.net. The most expensive are not always the best for you, but the cheapest is not what you want.

Networks in a small area are always competing for access. There are few usable channels for Wi-Fi, so there is always competition for access. I can tell you from experience this is true. I lived in the country; we had a big lot with no neighbors close. When I looked at the networks I could see, there was only mine. I had no issues with Wi-Fi kicking me off or not working. The 2.4 ghz was always fast and great.

We moved to a townhouse in a much more populated area. I can now see many networks when I look at the networks in my area. This extra traffic makes it important that your router is working at its best. It also needs to be using the least congested channels. This is one area where 5ghz Wi-Fi can improve your Wi-Fi. 5 ghz has more usable channels and a lot less traffic. There are 11 usable channels in the 2.4 ghz band. Everyone on that band is sharing those 11 channels. On the 5ghz band there are 45 usable channels. Using the highway analogy again it is like having 4 times as many lanes to drive in. Use the 5 ghz whenever you can.

Make sure your router is up to date. If you rent a router from your ISP, call them, and see if there is a newer router you can upgrade to. If you own your own, you should get the newer ones when they come out. New ones will come with all the latest security and the fastest speeds. It will also have the bands to give you the best performance in your home.

Research on the Internet if you are getting your own router. You can get a general feel of which are the best for what you want it to do for you. Performance can also differ from house to house, there is no one size fits all router.

Search the Internet for the best wireless routers. Check known sites that review this equipment. Such as PCmag, cnet, and consumer reports. Read the articles that go through the things to consider before buying your router.

Read their reviews and then go to websites like Amazon or Newegg and read buyer reviews. Make your decision on these things depending on your needs. This research will give the most up-to-date features and performance on routers.

Search on Google and when the search comes up, go to search tools. Select past month to get the latest up-to-date info. I ran one and found reviews and comparisons from this week going over the best wireless routers.

Prices on routers vary by several hundred dollars depending on what you want the router to do. So, doing the research is critical if cost is important. Make sure you are not looking at reviews over a year old, the technology has changed.

The 802.11n and 802.11ac are the latest and fastest routers available. Some of the new ac routers also contain a technology called beam forming. This helps strengthen your signal where you need it. It concentrates the signal in a beam to where you are using it, instead of all over the whole area. There is a new frequency that is brand new. The router is an 802.11ax. The ad is a 6ghz band.

The new 6ghz band is faster. This is called wi-fi 6E. As of now, there are a few laptops that support this technology, but few devices can even access it now.

Since I wrote this originally the standards for wi-fi naming have completely changed. This is creating a lot of confusion over what these names mean. The new listing for wi-fi will be.

- 802.11n is now wi-fi 4.
- 802.11ac is now wi-fi 5. This is not 5G and is not the 5ghz wi-fi band. This has created a lot of confusion in the terms.
- 802.11ax is wi-fi 6. Wi-fi 6 that uses the 6ghz band is 6E.

Wi-fi 6 is cool because it does have faster speed, but the main advantage to it is that it is smarter. Wi-fi 6 promises a speed increase of 30% which is certainly a bonus. What the smarter part is, and why it is faster is because it is set up to be much better at monitoring and directing multiple streams of data at the same time. The more devices that are connected to it the more efficient it is. It will direct the best signal to each device depending on what it is needing.

It will also pack more information into the packets it is sending. So instead of having 500 people in 500 cars on a single stretch of highway going down say 4 lanes, it will have those same 500 people going down the 4 lanes in 10 busses. Much less congestion and everything moves faster. Many fewer crashes.

The prices of the wi-fi 6 routers are now down in the affordable range. Xfinity newest xb7 router modem is wi-fi 6 certified. Check with your ISP if you rent from them to see if theirs is. You will not see as much benefit from a network that has one or two devices as you will with lots of devices from the wi-fi 6. As I said though, if you get your own, get the best you can afford to increase the life of the device.

Phones that support wi-fi 6 are the iPhone SE, and iPhone 11 and 12 and all models in the future. Also, Samsung galaxy S10, note 10 and S20 and S21 and all future models. There are a few others that support it now but for some reason none of the Pixel phone do as of now. Most of the new phones coming out in 2021 by the top makers will also support the wi-fi 6E. That will have the 6ghz channel as well. This is not 5G, that is something different that has nothing to do with wi-fi.

Other benefits are improved battery life on battery devices and better security encryption to keep you safe. Now that the prices have come down, there is not a reason not to get wi-fi 6 if you are replacing a router.

The extra speed comes with a reduction in range with the wi-fi 6E. The faster speed band has a higher frequency, but it has a shorter range. It is like the difference between the 2.4ghz and the 5ghz. The 5 is faster but it has a shorter range.

If your router has external antennas, it is possible to get better coverage by adjusting them. If set vertical you will get the best coverage in a flat plane out from the router. If you want the signal to go up or down, adjust the antennas in different directions. This will give coverage in all directions from the router. If the antennas are removable, you can replace them with higher gain antennas. The longer the antenna the higher the gain. That will give you a better range for your wi-fi signal.

You can change the channel your router is using to help increase speed if your router is older. Most N and AC routers, wi-fi 4 and wi-fi 5, will pick the best channel available when they connect. Let them do their own thing for the least interference. The problem changing the channel yourself is that next time that may not be the best channel. You will need to do it every time you get online to always be on the best channel.

EXTENDING YOUR WIFI

There are several types of Wi-Fi extenders you can use to improve your network. Some help a bit. Some help a lot. Regular Wi-Fi extenders that take the signal and amplify it will give you some help. You should expect to get about half of the signal of Wi-Fi coming from your router or less.

Power line adapters are a great alternative for hard-to-reach places. They work well from one side to the other where nothing else will reach. They are easy to hook up and will get you a good stable signal for a decent price. They use the existing house wiring to send the signal. You need at least two adapters.

You need to plug one into the router and the other into the outlet where you want to access it. You can get them with or without a pass-through plug. Get the pass-through ones so you can use the outlet to plug in other electrical devices.

This is a much under used way of getting Internet throughout your house, but it is a highly effective way to do it. Because this uses wires that are throughout your house already, you need not do any wiring. The main reason this is not more popular is because people do not know it exists.

The key to how well this work depends a lot on a couple of different things. The main one is the age and condition of your house wiring. If your wiring is old and not in good condition, you may not get much benefit. If there is good wiring in your house, you can get great results from these devices.

After the first connection, you can add more connections. You only need to add extra remote boxes, the others will work off the main one. The current standard will support up to 16 adapters on the same connection.

Make sure you use the security encryption. This makes sure your power-line adapters will not get tapped into. Noise from appliances can cause problems. Most of the adapters contain noise filters to stop this. Make sure the ones you get contain the noise filters.

Some power line adaptor answers and tips.
You can use them with a Mac or Windows, no issues.

- You can add a switch at the end to hook up more devices to the outer adaptors.
- You can also add another router or an access point at the far end to improve your wireless and wired network.
- Once you have the initial connection to your main router, you can add more adaptors. Up to 16, to extend it all over the house with your power lines. The huge benefit to this type of system it you get a connection on each adaptor like a direct ethernet connection to your router, so you do not have to run new wires all over your house.

An access point. There are access point options. These use another router to send your signal from a different location. The best way to do this is to run an Ethernet cable, or a power line adaptor to the area of your house where the service is not good. Plug the Ethernet cable into the power line adaptor, then into the access point router. Or if you run an ethernet cable, plug the ethernet cable into the access point at that location.

This will use the signal coming from your main router. It will send out another Wi-Fi signal from that point to Wi-Fi devices. This will extend your Wi-Fi coverage to that area of the house where it was not usable before. It will have a new network or 2 if you get a dual band access point. When I did this at my townhouse, I had 2 2.4ghz networks and 2 5ghz networks in my house. I could use all 4 of them for different device connections.

Wi-Fi range extenders.
These devices can give you some help in getting your signal out farther. I am not impressed with how well they work. From my experience, they give you a minimal benefit. They are easy to set up. You can move them to different parts of the house. I tried a couple different ones, and I saw no real improvement from them. They are inexpensive but there is not enough benefit to make them worth the cost.

The best way to use these devices is to stack them. Put the first one close to your router, the next one farther out and so on until you get to where the service is bad. What they do is pick up the Wi-Fi signal and amplify it and send it back out. One problem is they are not directional.

You cannot point the signal where you want it to go. So, everyone you set up has the same signal sent out in all directions. This can cause big overlaps which can interfere and make your Wi-Fi worse.

At the time of the original writing, there were some new whole home Wi-Fi systems called mesh systems. There are several of them now. Eero is the name of the first one available. From all the reviews I have read and from what I have seen, it works well. The prices have come down substantially from when I first wrote this. The prices are affordable now for a mesh system. As you can probably tell I have Xfinity internet. I have added the Xfinity pods to my home network. This is Xfinity's version of a mesh system and I have been incredibly happy with the added benefit from the mesh setup.

The difference between the mesh system and the extenders is huge. In simplest terms the mesh system has multiple routers that talk to each other and monitor where signal is needed, and they send it to that area. A mesh system gives you by far the best option to wirelessly get good signal all over your house. One way you can tell how it works is by doing speed tests in different places with your cell phone. I can see what the signal is in a particular part of the house. Then move the pod to a different outlet and test it.

When I set up my system of the main router and 3 pods, I had to move a couple of the pods a couple of times to get the best coverage all over the house. It took me about half an hour to get them into the optimum places for the best coverage. It is now set up, so I automatically connect to the 2.4ghz or the 5ghz depending on what the device supports and get the best signal everywhere in my house. I do not have to log into the different wi-fi bands. The system does it for me. This is where the mesh system shines.

BEST SOLUTIONS

In this section I will give you the exact setup I used in my townhouse to fix all my Internet problems. I have tried many things to improve my Internet. Some of them worked somewhat. Some did not work at all. This works fantastic. This is the setup I used at my previous house. This was before the mesh systems. At the time this was by far the best option, and for the money it is still an exceptionally good option if you cannot afford a mesh system.

I used the power-line adapters and an extra router to kick my system into overdrive. Here is the setup I was fighting with. I have my modem and router in an upstairs office. I wanted it there because that is where my desktop pc is where I do most of my most taxing Internet usage.

The problem was that the service in the main level of my house was not great. It was usable for email and general surfing but not great. I got 200 mbps on the machine in the office. I was getting 10 to 20 mbps in the main level. It was not consistent either. So streaming was an issue and even using my laptop for writing, I would lose connection. I am sure many of you have similar issues that frustrate you.

After setting this up I had an Ethernet connection in my main level where I use my laptop, I get a steady 85 mbps. I also had 5 ghz Wi-Fi in my main level at 45 to 60 mbps, and another 2.4 ghz network at 40 mbps, plus my original connection.

Here is what I did. I got two powerline adapters, a switch, and an extra router repeater. I put one power line adapter near my modem and plugged in an Ethernet cable. I put the other power line adapter where I wanted the hard-wired connection in the main level. I plugged an Ethernet cable into the second power line adapter and plugged it into a 5-port switch.

I plugged an Ethernet cable from the switch and into my laptop. I then plugged another Ethernet cable into the switch. Set the router-to-router position and plugged it in. This little router gets the strong signal from the power line adapter. It puts out the Wi-Fi signals for my main level.

I then changed my fire stick on the living room TV to the 5ghz network from the second router. I can stream with the 5 ghz band to the fire stick no

problem. This is easy to setup and works fantastic.
Here are the items I used.

Power line adapters I do not know that these
are any better than others. However, they have the
pass-through plug that does not cover the other
outlet. You are not giving up any outlets to use this
set up.

Switch You can get much bigger one if you need
more ports. The 5 port was plenty for me.

Router You can use any compatible router, the
one I used at the time is no longer available but this
one will work fine.

The cool thing about this setup is that you can add
up to 16 power line adapters. You can add more
routers as well to cover any size house. For the
power line adapters, it says they work best if on the
same circuit. I am sure it works better on the same
circuit.

It works fine through your box and on different
circuits in the same wiring system. If it were on the
same circuit, it could get over 100mbps, but I was
more than happy with being in the 60 plus range.

If you are having problems streaming video on your TV. And you have a box like a roku with an Ethernet connection. Put a power line adapter behind your TV and plug your roku in and you will never have trouble streaming again.

SUMMARY

You can try some of the different options I have
covered throughout this book. Some of them work
and help some. The best option for the lowest cost
is the option in my best solutions section. If getting
the best coverage in all parts of your house is your
goal, this is the way to do it for the lowest cost. This
set up cost me about $140, but it is money well
spent. I can do all the things I want in all parts of
my house without the dropped connections and no
spotty service. The cost for doing this setup is now
even less.

The great thing is that you can add up to 15 more
adapters to the system. You can have a direct wire
connection to every room in your house. Everyone
can plug in their computer and gaming systems to
avoid Wi-Fi issues. And if they all need better Wi-Fi
also, add a low-cost router to boost the Wi-Fi into
the areas with low signal.

The mesh system may be the easiest answer to your
issues, but there is a higher startup cost to it. If cost
is not an issue for you, and most of the devices you
are using are wi-fi the mesh is the way to go. If you
want to have a wired connection in ever room and

do not want to re wire your house, use the powerline adaptor setup.

If you have questions, or need help with any of this, you can email me, and I will get back to you as soon as possible. **Steve@stevepease.net**

If the information is helpful, please go to the Amazon site and leave a review of the book. **Amazon website.** Thanks again for reading my book.

ABOUT ME

My name is Steve Pease. I live in the Northern suburbs of the Twin Cities in Minnesota.

I started writing about six years ago. I have written several hundred articles for Hub pages and for examiner over the years. For Examiner I wrote a column for the Twin Cities on Disc golf. I also wrote a column on Cycling in the Twin Cities, and one on Exercise and fitness for the Twin cities.

I write on subjects I am passionate about. Disc golf, exercise, photography, cycling, fishing, and topics that deal with Christian beliefs.

My father is a retired minister, and he has written many books. I have edited many of them and have them available on my site. they cover many topics of interest to Christians today.

I have been playing disc golf since 1978 and love the sport. The greatest thing about disc golf is at age fifty-eight, I am still competitive. I beat players much younger than me. Disc golf is a sport you can play at almost any age if you can walk.

I have taken several hundred thousand pictures over the last 35 years. I am trying to improve my photography every day. My goal is always to take the best shots I can. I want people to say wow when they look at my shots. I went through the photography course at New York Institute of photography. What I have learned from the course, and my years of experience was worth every dollar.

The key to being a great photographer is to see things that most people do not see, or in a way they did not see it. My favorite types of photography are landscapes, portraits, animals and infrared. I have shot several weddings. I have also spent hundreds of hours exploring different places. Always looking for great things to take pictures of.

I have been an avid fisherman since I was a kid. I have had two bass fishing boats over the years, but I enjoy fishing for my kayak. I have a sit inside old town kayak and a sit on top feel free Moken 12 fishing kayak. I also have two old town canoes for going to the Boundary Waters Canoe Area Wilderness. We also go paddling around lakes in my area.

  The hardest part about fishing from a kayak is trying to decide what not to take with me. As with most bass fishermen I have tons of equipment, and I always feel I need to take it all with me in case I need it. Kayak fishing has made me downsize to make everything fit in my kayak.

I spend most of my fishing time catching bass and northern pike. But if I am looking for a good meal, you can beat crappies and sunfish. I have spent most of my time fishing freshwater, but I have caught saltwater fish. The biggest was a 380-pound bull shark off Key West Florida in 1985.

I have also loved biking and exercising since I was in my early teens. I like to read nonfiction books so I can keep learning new things all the time. Many of the things I learn I want to share with you and help enrich your life. I want to pass on the knowledge I have learned over the years so that others can share my knowledge.

Thanks again.

Check out my book site for other good books.
Stevepease.net